White Fear

Taylor Dyer

Guide to How Browning of American is Making White Folks Loss their minds

In 1963, the U.S. Commission on Civil Rights dispatched a document to President John F. Kennedy and congressional leaders, concluding: "It is now one hundred years seeing that this kingdom, lagging in the back of different civilized countries, abolished slavery. Yet nowadays, the descendants of these freed slaves nevertheless be afflicted by customs, traditions and prejudices that need to have died with the group wherein they flourished."

Five years later, President Lyndon Johnson's National Advisory Commission on Civil Disorders -- typically called the Kerner Commission after its chair, Gov. Otto Kerner of Illinois -- issued its document at the reasons of and destiny treatments for the race-associated disturbances that had swept the kingdom all through the preceding year. The document famously concluded that "our kingdom is transferring in the direction of societies, one black, one white -- separate and unequal" and argued that without dramatic action, the kingdom could see a "persevering with polarization of the American network and, ultimately, the destruction of simple democratic values."

In June 1997, President Bill Clinton introduced a sweeping Initiative on Race, announcing: "I ask the American human beings to sign up for me in a first-rate country wide attempt to ideal the promise of America for this new time as we are searching for to construct our extra ideal union. ... That is the incomplete paintings of our time, to raise the weight of race and redeem the promise of America."

Decades prior, in 1939, Dr. George Gallup had protected in his surveys a query approximately race -- as Gallup's Justin McCarthy said in his review, "the primary time Gallup had polled on any difficulty associated with race or racism." The query focused at the controversy surrounding first female Eleanor Roosevelt's resignation from the Daughters of the American Revolution while that company refused to permit Marian Anderson, a famous black opera singer, carry out in certainly considered one among its halls. (The majority of Americans, 57%, accepted of Roosevelt's resignation, even as 28% disapproved and 15% had no opinion.) As Dr. Gallup found out the ones a few years ago, polling furnished a uniquely critical feature with the aid of using supporting positioned race troubles with inside the context of the attitudes and ideals of common Americans -- and in precise, the ones of black Americans.

There isn't any extra critical time to offer this context than now, because the kingdom another time is centered at the implications of the racial divides and racial inequalities which have been part of this kingdom's cloth basically seeing that its founding.

There has certainly been a massive quantity of polling on race members of the family (with the aid of using Gallup and lots of different organizations) -- and over the years, the outcomes had been ably collected, analyzed and summarized. In reviewing this studies, I come away with 3 simple conclusions:

Blacks in America nowadays keep to document dwelling a lifestyle wherein they confront bias and discrimination on nearly all fronts.

Americans aren't any extra high quality approximately race members of the family nowadays than they had been in many years beyond, and in a few times are much less high quality nowadays.

There is a giant hole among whites' and blacks' perceptions of the location of blacks in U.S. society.

Black Americans Living a Life of Discrimination and Unequal Opportunity

Data from Gallup and lots of different survey reasserts verify that majorities of black Americans document dwelling a lifestyle wherein they confront bias, discrimination, fewer possibilities to get in advance and persevering with confrontations with prejudice.

I reviewed tons of those information final year.

"Only 18% of blacks are happy with the manner blacks are handled on this us of a nowadays, as compared with 51% of whites who say they're happy with the manner blacks are handled. Well over 1/2 of blacks trust that blacks are handled much less favorably than whites in managing police, in shops and malls, and at the job. About

1/2 of blacks say blacks are handled much less favorably in community shops, in eating places and in getting healthcare. More than one in 5 black Americans say that withinside the final 30 days, they had been handled unfairly in shops, in eating places or with the aid of using the police. Slightly fewer, however nevertheless giant numbers, say that they've been handled unfairly at paintings or in receiving healthcare. A moderate majority of blacks are pessimistic approximately the destiny, announcing that members of the family among blacks and whites will usually be a hassle on this us of a."

Pew Research located comparable outcomes of their document on race attitudes final year. Over 8 in 10 blacks of their look at stated blacks are handled much less pretty than whites with the aid of using the crook justice system, in managing police, and in hiring, pay and promotions. Seven in 10 or extra stated they had been handled much less pretty while making use of for a mortgage or loan and even as in shops and eating places. Pew's studies additionally located 60% to 65% of blacks announcing that due to their race, human beings had acted like they had been suspicious of them or acted like they notion they had been now no longer smart. And a current Pew look at located that 83% of blacks stated that they'd skilled discrimination or been handled unfairly due to their race or ethnicity.

Of precise relevance given current activities are the findings displaying that black Americans document unequal and discriminatory remedy with the aid of using police. Specifically, 77% of blacks in Gallup's 2018 ballot stated that blacks are handled much less pretty than whites with the aid of using police, and 21% said being handled unfairly with the aid of using police withinside the beyond 30 days.

There had been current updates. A CBS News ballot carried out in overdue May and early June confirmed that 83% of blacks say police are much more likely to apply lethal pressure in opposition to blacks than in opposition to whites, and that 44% of blacks say police of their network lead them to feel "primarily anxious" alternatively than "primarily safe." The current Pew Research ballot confirmed that 45% of blacks document having been unfairly stopped with the aid of using police due to their race or ethnicity.

A current Monmouth University survey confirmed that 87% of blacks trust police are much more likely to apply immoderate pressure if the offender is black -- and that simply 21% of blacks are "very happy" with their neighborhood police department, as compared with 45% of whites.

General attitudes about race have become more negative Americans' perceptions of the racial situation in American society have not improved in recent decades and, in many cases, have become even more negative.

High expectations were placed on race relations during the early Obama administration, with more than two-thirds of Americans saying his election was the most important or one of two or three important steps forward. most important to blacks in more than 100 years. By the end of his administration, however, attitudes about race had deteriorated rather than improved.

As Gallup's Mohamed Youngish wrote last year: "Since 2013, Americans' generally positive perceptions of race have cooled, and perceptions of blacks have deteriorated significantly. This period of decline has seen police shootings. involving black citizens, a neo-Nazi protest and the violence that followed Charlottesville, Va., and racist attacks on a black house of worship in Charleston, South Carolina. All of these events have captured national attention and made the challenge of race relations a priority for Americans."

And things certainly didn't improve in the early years of the Trump administration. Every survey I know gives President Donald Trump a low score on his handling of race relations, and Trump's job approval rate for blacks remains below 20%.

In 2018, about half of all Americans rated the relationship between whites and blacks as "good," down significantly from 70% or more, who previously rated the relationship as good. And in 2019, 40% of Americans said they were "very" worried about race relations, following a number of high-profile cases involving police shootings of unarmed black people and a number of cases. white policemen are black criminals. This is up significantly from 13% in 2010. (The percentage of Americans concerned about race relations in this year's March update, prior to recent events, has dropped to 31%).

Some Gallup trends reflect the growing negativity in black attitudes over the years. Just over half of blacks agreed in 1995 that blacks are as likely to get any job as whites; By 2018, that number had dropped to 30%. That same year, four out of 10 blacks agreed they had an equal opportunity for housing, the lowest level of Gallup's trend. And blacks' views of being treated fairly in the workplace, in stores, restaurants and bars, and by the police are the lowest Gallup has measured. On the other hand, most self-reports of unfair treatment in the past 30 days are similar to what happened in 1997 when these measures were implemented.

Not all trends turn negative. In the general population, there have been lasting changes in two basic attitudes about race. The percentage of Americans who say they would vote for another qualified black president has increased to 96%, from 38% in 1958. And the percentage of

Americans who approve of a marriage between Blacks and whites increased from 48% in 1965 to 87% when Gallup last updated the measure in 2013.

White people describe a different reality than black people

Gallup has regularly asked whites to answer similar questions about racism as asked against blacks, and the results consistently show that whites are less likely to perceive prejudice. and discriminate against blacks more than blacks themselves. In short, black and white Americans see the world through different lenses, with blacks describing a much more difficult set of experiences than whites perceive.

For example, 30% of blacks versus 67% of whites believe that blacks are about as likely as whites to get any kind of job for which they are qualified, and we found similar differences in views on housing and education. Whites and blacks also differ on the notion that blacks are treated less fairly in the workplace, shopping, in bars and restaurants, getting health care, and dealing with the police. Just over half of whites are satisfied with the way blacks are treated in society, but only 18% of blacks agree. Fifty-four percent of whites say the relationship between whites and blacks is good, compared with 40 percent of blacks.

Additionally, Gallup's June update found that whites (15%) are less likely than blacks (45%) to consider race relations the most important issue facing the nation.

In 2018, about half of all Americans rated the relationship between whites and blacks as "good," down significantly from 70% or more, who previously rated the relationship as good. And in 2019, 40% of Americans said they were "very" worried about race relations, following a number of high-profile cases involving police shootings of unarmed black people and a number of cases.

white policemen are black criminals. This is up significantly from 13% in 2010. (The percentage of Americans concerned about race relations in this year's March update, prior to recent events, has dropped to 31%).

Some Gallup trends reflect the growing negativity in black attitudes over the years. Just over half of blacks agreed in 1995 that blacks are as likely to get any job as whites; By 2018, that number had dropped to 30%. That same year, four out of 10 blacks agreed they had an equal opportunity for housing, the lowest level of Gallup's trend. And blacks' views of being treated fairly in the workplace, in stores, restaurants and bars, and by the police are the lowest Gallup has measured. On the other hand, most self-reports of unfair treatment in the past 30 days are similar to what happened in 1997 when these measures were implemented.

Not all trends turn negative. In the general population, there have been lasting changes in two basic attitudes about race. The percentage of Americans who say they would vote for another qualified black president has increased to 96%, from 38% in 1958. And the percentage of Americans who approve of a marriage between Blacks and whites increased from 48% in 1965 to 87% when Gallup last updated the measure in 2013.

White people describe a different reality than black people

Gallup has regularly asked whites to answer similar questions about racism as asked against blacks, and the results consistently show that whites are less likely to perceive prejudice. and discriminate against blacks more than blacks themselves. In short, black and white Americans see the world through different lenses, with blacks describing a much more difficult set of experiences than whites perceive.

For example, 30% of blacks versus 67% of whites believe that blacks are about as likely as whites to get any kind of job for which they are qualified, and we found similar differences in views on housing and education. Whites and blacks also differ on the notion that blacks are treated less fairly in the workplace, shopping, in bars and restaurants, getting health care, and dealing with the police. Just over half of whites are satisfied with the way blacks are treated in society, but only 18% of blacks agree. Fifty-four percent of whites say the relationship between whites and blacks is good, compared with 40 percent of blacks.

Additionally, Gallup's June update found that whites (15%) are less likely than blacks (45%) to consider race relations the most important issue facing the nation.

There were many, many new packages, organizations and commissions centered at the race trouble over time for the reason that landmark civil rights regulation of the 1960s. Yet our survey information informs us that among the equal troubles recognized many years in the past are nonetheless with us, and that black Americans continue to be in a scenario they outline as starkly much less same than the only going through whites.

It is one thing, of course, to file the terrible approaches wherein blacks in America these days understand the demanding situations they face of their day by day lives. It is some other to determine out what must be finished approximately it.

The information display that black Americans need the federal authorities to be concerned and they suppose new legal guidelines and rules addressing race problems are wished. As I summarized closing year:

"Black Americans additionally truly accept as true with that authorities moves must be taken to assist result in change. Over seven in 10 blacks prefer affirmative motion packages for racial minorities on this us of a, and a majority of 57% of whites agree. Previous Gallup studies has proven that approximately -thirds of black Americans accept as true with the U.S. authorities must play a main position in looking to enhance the social and financial role of blacks and different minority corporations on this us of a. Over seven in 10 blacks accept as true with that new civil rights legal guidelines are wished on this us of a to lessen discrimination towards blacks."

Additionally, maximum polls I`ve reviewed display that a majority of blacks guide the idea of reparations, with variant in that stage of guide relying on how the query is asked. (Wording is crucial due to the fact the idea of reparations has many definitions and implications, relying on who's presenting it.) The maximum latest country wide survey I'm conscious of, performed via way of means of the Associated Press/NORC closing fall, determined that 74% of blacks agreed that the U.S. federal authorities must "pay reparations for slavery and racial discrimination on this us of a via way of means of making coins bills to the descendants of enslaved people." (Only 15% of whites agreed.)

Certainly, finishing police brutality and unwarranted concentrated on of blacks is a criminal imperative, and there's a clean want for broader societal popularity of the systemic racism in U.S. society suggested via way of means of blacks for generations. There have been a few upticks in Gallup's information in the proportion of whites who understand that blacks are dealt with much less pretty at work, even as shopping, at bars and restaurants, in getting healthcare, and in handling police -- even though maximum of those possibilities have been nonetheless low in Gallup's modern day replace years in the past. Recent polling performed via way of means of different corporations suggests large will increase in whites' perceptions that racism and discrimination constitute a huge trouble for the use of an and that blacks are dealt with unfairly.

Overall, as is the case with maximum urgent social and financial problems, there's a clean want for management on race withinside the U.S., as there was for the loads of years wherein race has been a defining American Dilemma. There are requires renewed "get out the vote" efforts on the neighborhood and country wide levels, with the desire that new leaders might be capable of result in lasting change. Additionally, the seeming seriousness with which Americans of all races have reacted to the modern day incidents of police brutality towards blacks may also sign that this time the scenario is different -- and that as a result, the kingdom may also see greater large development in addressing the kingdom's race-associated demanding situations going forward. Future Gallup updates of middle race family members fashion questions might be crucial signs of the diploma to which latest activities have or have now no longer had a remarkable effect on Americans' perspectives on race.

Most Remain Optimistic for Better Future

Although rankings of the present day country of black-white family members, amongst all Americans in addition to blacks and whites, have fallen sharply due to the fact 2013, their reviews approximately whether or not black-white family members will usually be a hassle for the U.S. were stable. Since 2002, as a minimum 1/2 of of Americans have persisted to mention family members among blacks and whites will finally be labored out. Currently, 57% accept as true with this, at the same time as 39% assume that black-white family members will usually be a hassle for the U.S. The excessive factor in optimism, 67% "finally labored out," got here in a ballot performed the night time after Barack Obama`s election as president in 2008.

Notably, the Nineties continue to be the maximum pessimistic decade on black-white family members withinside the U.S.; at that time, majorities continuously expected that such family members might usually be a hassle for the country. This length coincided with racially charged occasions that captured the nation's interest, which include the L.A. race riots and the O.J. Simpson trial.

Yet, further to checks of present day race family members, the dearth of extrude in expectancies nationally mask a considerable variance among white and black respondents. Most blacks (53%) say family members among blacks and whites will usually be a hassle, at the same time as 38% of non-Hispanic white's percentage this view.

Black women (55%) are statistically as probable as black men (52%) to look such family members as usually being a hassle for the U.S. Perhaps as a signal of the pervasive nature of the mission, black respondent's elderly 50 and older (58%) have a better probability than the ones elderly 18-49 (51%) to view family members among blacks and whites as usually posing a hassle for the country.

Implications

When one compares Americans' perspectives of race family members amongst maximum racial groups, they're maximum divided on black-white family members. Although a majority of Americans describe the present day country of black-white family members as appropriate and specific optimism that demanding situations among the races could be finally labored out, black Americans describe present day family members among whites and blacks as both very or fairly awful at the very best degrees of this century.

Immediately after the election of the primary black U.S. president, Americans' optimism approximately the destiny of black-white family members soared. However, due to the fact 2013, Americans' average fantastic perceptions on race have cooled, and perceptions amongst blacks have soured considerably. This length of decline has witnessed excessive-profile police capturing incidents regarding black citizens, a neo-Nazi rally and resulting violence in Charlottesville, Virginia, and racially charged assaults on a black residence of worship in Charleston, South Carolina. All of those occasions captured the countrywide interest and feature saved the mission of race family members at the leading edge of Americans' minds.

Americans Slow to Back Interracial Marriage

Fifty years in the past this month, the U.S. Supreme Court dominated in Loving v. Virginia that a Virginia ban on marriage among whites and blacks became unconstitutional, accordingly putting down such legal guidelines anywhere they existed withinside the country. In strengthen of this ruling, Gallup determined the American public calmly split: 48% of U.S. adults in January 1965 accredited of legal guidelines making marriage among blacks and whites a crime, at the same time as 46% disapproved.

At the time of the ballot, 19 states had legal guidelines in opposition to marriage among whites and blacks, inclusive of all sixteen states which are normally taken into consideration a part of the South. Accordingly, the ballot determined sharp local variations in this query. Most Southern whites accredited of the legal guidelines, at the same time as the moderate majority of non-Southern whites disapproved.

The authentic Gallup information launch additionally suggested that almost 3 in 10 Southern blacks, as opposed to one in seven blacks residing outdoor the South, desired legal guidelines making marriage among whites and blacks a crime.

U.S. Opposition Was an Outlier Among Western Nations

A query from a 1968 global Gallup ballot underscores the quantity of U.S. competition to interracial marriage for the duration of this period. This query, which requested Americans and people in 12 different international locations whether or not they individually accredited or disapproved of marriage among whites and nonwhites, determined even broader U.S. competition than the 1965 query.

More than seven in 10 Americans (72%) disapproved of white-nonwhite marriages, in evaluation with most effective 21% of citizens in Sweden, 23% withinside the Netherlands, 25% in France, 34% in Finland, 35% in Switzerland and 36% in Greece.

Opposition outweighed guide in Austria, Canada, West Germany, Norway, Uruguay and Great Britain, however to a much lesser quantity than withinside the U.S.

The 1965 and 1968 U.S. reactions to interracial marriage seem contradictory, however that is due to the fact every query measures a special measurement of public opinion. The 1965 query asks for people's perspectives at the legality of interracial marriage -- whether or not it ought to be a crime -- while the 1968 query simply asks Americans whether or not they individually approve.

Americans' non-public perspectives on interracial marriage ultimately changed, however it took a long time for majority guide to emerge. In 1978, greater than a decade after the Loving case, most effective 36% of Americans accredited, at the same time as 54% nonetheless disapproved. Not till the Nineteen Nineties did public approval pass the 50% threshold, registering 64% in 1997. Gallup's present day update, in 2013, suggests 87% approving.

Community Influences on White Racial Attitudes: What Matters and Why?

Tracing the roots of racial attitudes in historic activities and man or woman biographies has been a longstanding aim of race members of the family scholars. Recent years have visible a brand new improvement in racial mindset studies: Local network context has entered the highlight as a capability effect on racial perspectives. The race composition of the locality has been the maximum not unusual place focus; proof from in advance many years indicates that white Americans are much more likely to preserve anti-black attitudes in the event that they stay in regions in which the African American populace is enormously large. However, an influential 2000 article argued that the socioeconomic composition of the white network is an extra effective effect on white attitudes: In low-SES locales, "stress-inducing" deprivations and hardships in whites' personal lives purportedly make them disparage blacks. The observe stated right here re-assesses this "scapegoating" claim, the usage of statistics from the 1998–2002 General Social Surveys connected to 2000 census statistics approximately groups. Across many dimensions of racial attitudes, there's suggested effect of each neighborhood racial proportions and university of entirety fees amongst white residents. However, the monetary measurement of SES exerts negligible effect on white racial attitudes, suggesting that neighborhood procedures apart from scapegoating have to be at work.

Studies of racial attitudes enhance extensive theoretical questions crucial to researchers in lots of branches of social science. However, perspectives approximately race aren't only a count number of scholarly interest: Public opinion can affect public policy (Burstein 2003), inclusive of race policy (Pride 2000). Traditional strategies to expertise racial attitudes appearance to the traits and situations of man or woman perceivers, in conjunction with extensive historic styles and activities. Recent years have visible a crucial extension of racial mindset studies, calling interest to the capability effect of neighborhood groups on residents` perspectives. Among network traits, frequently mentioned as "contextual" or "environmental" factors, race composition has been the maximum not unusual place focus. However, a few researchers argue that the socioeconomic composition of the neighborhood white network is the stronger contextual force. If there's debate approximately which environmental traits affect racial attitudes, even extra stays to be found out approximately how neighborhood procedures function mediators, reworking demographic styles into racial attitudes of white residents. This observe reviews proof approximately which network traits form racial attitudes, and considers implications of these findings for neighborhood mediating procedures.

Backdrop: The effect of neighborhood race composition

Theory and studies have pointed to neighborhood race composition, specially the share of African Americans withinside the populace, as an important effect on white racial attitudes. Previous research has discovered white Americans reporting extra race prejudice in localities in which the black populace percentage is high (see, for example, Fossett and Kiecolt 1989; Quillian 1996; Taylor 1998), specially out of doors the South (Taylor 1998). Tangible consequences which includes racial occupational inequality (Burr, Galle, and Fossett 1991) and reality of crook punishment (Liska, Chamlin, and Reed 1985) have additionally proven tremendous institutions with the relative length of the neighborhood African American populace, probably as an outgrowth of terrible white attitudes.

The proposition that white hostility can be fueled through proximity to racial minorities isn't always new (see All port 1954; Williams 1947). The underlying dynamic is frequently assumed to be chance related to a few shape of "sensible organization conflict" (Levine and Campbell 1972). Economic and political rivalries had been mentioned through Blalock (1967), who concluded that chance/opposition in every of those spheres produced a one-of-a-kind curvilinear dating among black numbers and white reactions: With monetary opposition, white antipathy must sharply boom as minority attention starts to upward thrust however degree off at better degrees of minority populace, through which factor whites have advanced mechanisms of exclusion to manipulate the monetary chance; political chance, in contrast, rises at an accelerating fee as minority numbers boom, and therefore so does white antipathy. Emphasizing monetary opposition, Quillian (1996) used nearby black populace percentage in conjunction with in step with capita earnings as a hallmark of "perceived organization chance," demonstrating that the previous relates immediately and the latter inversely to white prejudice and competition to race-targeting. Political battle has been the point of interest of analysts which includes Giles and his colleagues (see Giles and Evans 1985); for example, Giles and Hertz (1994) confirmed white Southerners` defections from the Democratic birthday celebration to be extra in which blacks had been closely represented withinside the neighborhood populace.

Perceived risk which can mediate consequences of black populace numbers on white attitudes want now no longer be completely financial or political.

Herbert Blumer (1958) portrayed white prejudice as a "experience of institution role" that will become virulent prejudice while the dominant role is threatened. The dynamic Blumer defined is frequently referenced in discussions of financial and political opposition, however may be interpreted as extra encompassing. Analysts with inside the Tajfel way of life describe in-institution identity and out-institution derogation as serving mental desires for social inclusion and distinctiveness (Tajfel and Turner 1986; Brewer 1991) or tries to hold social reputation and therefore self-esteem (see Forbes` dialogue of social identification theory, 1997:32). Followers of Blumer would possibly make a comparable factor however with a sociological twist, noting that the valued experience of dominant institution role is multifaceted, entailing diffuse social reputation alongside financial and political gains.

Indeed, doubtlessly essential sorts of risk aroused via way of means of the presence of minorities aren't exhausted while we upload reputation to the financial and political spheres. Whites` experience of bodily risk from minorities is emphasized with inside the crook justice literature; and objections to the inclusion of non-English languages in training and public existence are reminders that cultural risk can be essential, whether or not the minority in query is African Americans or Hispanics. Citing Liska (1992) amongst others, Stults and Baumer word that a few analysts agree with the presence of minorities might also additionally result in tightened social controls due to the fact "culturally assorted minority corporations are perceived as a diffuse risk to the social order" (2007:510).

A Different Focus: Socioeconomic composition of the white network

A provocative and influential article via way of means of Oliver and Mendelberg (2000) argues that in advance analysts were given the tale approximately environmental consequences on racial attitudes in general wrong. Black populace proportion has confined effect on white attitudes, those analysts claim, in large part due to the fact segregated establishments had been erected to mitigate racial opposition and risk. As helping proof, Oliver and Mendelberg record their 1991 smartphone survey findings that neither zip code-stage nor metropolitan-stage share black appears to affect "symbolic racism;" and that racial stereotyping is further unaffected via way of means of zip code-stage race composition, despite the fact that a modest courting exists on the metro stage. Overall, those researchers contend that network traits affect coverage reviews best wherein the particular predictor indexes opposition withinside the area referenced via way of means of the coverage query. Thus, for example, their statistics did proof a metropolitan-stage effect of share black on whites` reviews approximately affirmative movement in employment, purportedly due to the fact task opposition exists on the metropolitan stage.

The extra effective environmental effect on white citizens` racial attitudes, in step with Oliver and Mendelberg (2000), is the socioeconomic composition of the nearby white network. These researchers took the share of nearby whites keeping university levels as their contextual SES predictor and located zip code-stage consequences of this training index on measures of racial attitudes, internet of the effect of tutorial attainment via way of means of character white citizens.

In sociology in addition to political science, the Oliver and Mendelberg (2000) paper has obtained full-size attention – stated to valid the look for contextual consequences in general, even in tasks wherein the focal environmental predictor is the component that Oliver and Mendelberg downplayed, racial composition of the nearby populace (for example, see Dixon 2006; McLaren 2003). Among research which have targeted on socioeconomic reputation as an environmental effect on racial and different attitudes, more than a few have accompanied Oliver and Mendelberg in the use of academic stage of nearby citizens to symbolize SES (see Blake 2003; Branton and Jones 2005; Marschall and Stolle 2004; Soss, Langbein, and Metelko 2003).

Interpretation of socioeconomic composition outcomes

Why need to the socioeconomic composition of the neighborhood white network matter? Oliver and Mendelberg taken into consideration and rejected a listing of possibilities. If low SES neighborhood environments boom whites` feel of vulnerability, then low SES withinside the white network could enlarge the hazard represented with the aid of using neighborhood black numbers; in

Oliver and Mendelberg`s facts such interplay turned into absent. If the contextual SES degree contemplated the effect of sure unmeasured character differences, its pressure need to be faded with the aid of using introducing political statistics as a manipulate variable; their facts confirmed no such pattern. Social norms are an incredible mediator of the contextual SES impact, Oliver and Mendelberg contend, due to the fact citizens inside regions as big as zip codes don`t usually engage sufficient to broaden norms; additionally, zip code regions don`t contain "far-attaining normative institutions" (2000:585) that could generate sturdy norms, nor turned into the contextual SES impact greater suggested amongst longer-time period citizens, as a normative clarification may imply.

By elimination, Oliver and Mendelberg got here to prefer what others may call "scapegoating" principle to provide an explanation for the zip code-degree contextual SES outcomes emphasized of their findings. "The finest environmental determinants of racial attitudes come now no longer from fabric competition, social norms, or unmeasured character characteristics, however from mental responses of out-organization aversion which might be induced with the aid of using low fame contexts" (2000:586). The authors` introductory dialogue paved the manner for this conclusion: "Low-fame settings, described with the aid of using low fees of schooling and employment, disclose citizens to a day by day dose of petty crime, focused bodily decay and social disorder…This publicity in flip results in a constellation of poor mental states… In settings characterized with the aid of using trendy tension and fear, anti-black have an effect on might also additionally rise up due to the fact African Americans are a salient goal in a racially divided society" (2000: 576).

This portrayal intently echoes All port`s (1954) description of scapegoating. All port underlines "the escapist characteristic of aggressiveness…(its) potential to melt the disappointments and frustrations of lifestyles," and is going directly to say: "Throughout lifestyles the identical tendency persists for anger to middle upon to be had in preference to logical objects" (1954:343).

A very extraordinary interpretation is recommended if we consciousness now no longer on "socioeconomic" composition, however at the environmental SES degree honestly utilized in a lot of the present studies—the academic composition of the white network. For one thing, this invitations interest to methods which could exist in better-fame white communities, now no longer simply to the demoralization which could pervade the white populace of lower-fame communities.

A considerate and provocative interpretation of contextual schooling outcomes turned into spelled out with the aid of using Moore and Ovadia (2006) in reference to studies now no longer on racial attitudes, however on assist for civil liberties. Moore and Ovadia propose: "transmission of pro-tolerance attitudes that end result from more concentrations of university graduates is done thru institutional and macrosocial means, in place of the face-to-face interactions among comparable people." And they cross directly to say: "It can be that regions with greater university graduates are much more likely to by skip anti-discrimination laws (and can additionally be much more likely to look that they're enforced). These regions might also additionally have more potent norms of cultural attractiveness that lead each the university knowledgeable and people without stages to be accepting of non-normative people and their thoughts. Institutions, which include neighborhood governments, schools, cultural facilities and businesses, can be much more likely to create and assist pro-tolerance sports whilst the populace that they serve consists of a better percentage of people who are probably to fee diversity. And despite the fact that those public sports can be installation in reaction to the needs of the highbrow elite, their outcomes are probably to be felt all through the network" (2006:2215).

The mediation of socioeconomic composition outcomes has but to acquire the educational attention given to mediation of race composition outcomes on racial attitudes, making those Moore and Ovadia thoughts a particularly treasured contribution.

THE PRESENT STUDY

An imperative cognizance of this studies is the have an impact on of socioeconomic composition withinside the nearby white network at the racial attitudes of its citizens. In particular, we are trying to find to disentangle the have an impact on of white academic composition from that of white monetary composition to be able to adjudicate among change interpretations of discovered environmental SES outcomes. As well, we reply to in advance comparisons of white socioeconomic composition with race composition outcomes via way of means of along with nearby racial proportions amongst our key predictors.

More especially, having related 1998–2002 General Social Survey (GSS) responses to facts from the 2000 U.S. Census approximately the localities in which the GSS respondents live, we ask:

1) In those information, what's the proof that black populace proportion withinside the metropolitan vicinity or non-metro county affects white racial attitudes?

Research the use of 1990 GSS information confirmed noteworthy metropolitan-stage outcomes of the percentage of citizens who had been African American (Taylor 1998). Oliver and Mendelberg (2000) de-emphasized race composition outcomes, reporting inconsistent metropolitan-stage proportion-black outcomes throughout their racial mindset and 3 racial coverage measures. However, the Oliver and Mendelberg studies used dummy variables in place of a non-stop scale to index race composition, and brought controls—zip code-stage contextual variables and political celebration affiliation—that can distort the evaluation of metro-stage predictors. An up to date evaluation is needed, the use of a non-stop race composition predictor and a wide array of 8 racial mindset measures.

2) To what volume are the racial attitudes of white citizens tormented by the instructional composition of the white network withinside the metropolitan vicinity or non-metropolitan county?

The influential Oliver and Mendelberg article assessed the effect of contextual training simplest on the zip code stage, assuming that the variety of instructional composition throughout metropolitan regions is simply too small and the variety inside sub-groups of metropolitan regions too extraordinary for metro-stage training to be a manageable have an impact on racial attitudes (2000: 577). Our undertaking checks that assumption.

3) To what volume are the racial attitudes of white citizens tormented by the monetary composition of the white network withinside the metropolitan vicinity or non-metropolitan county?

This undertaking dissects white "socioeconomic" composition, assessing the function of monetary context in addition to academic context. What is the relative energy of white academic and monetary composition while every is tested separately, and does every issue of combination SES make a contribution to know-how white racial attitudes while each are blanketed in multivariate analyses?

Why cognizance on White Americans` attitudes approximately blacks? The want to evaluate outgroup attitudes amongst perceivers aside from European Americans and for goals aside from African Americans is crucially essential in our multiracial society (see, for example, Taylor and Schroeder 2010). However, there are clean indicators that black goals face especially disparaging attitudes (see, for example, Bobo and Hutchings 1996; Dixon 2006). And there is strong proof that the effect of minority populace proportions differs while the minority organization is blacks in place of Hispanics or Asians (see, for example, Taylor 1998; Taylor and Aurand 2004; Dixon 2006). Furthermore, the interplay of racial context with person interracial revel in relies upon on which minority organization is the cognizance (Dixon 2006). In short, poor attitudes held via way of means of whites approximately blacks are especially acute, and environmental effects on the ones attitudes are in a few approaches unique. Even as treasured studies related to different perceivers and goals is pursued, there's adequate motive to invite especially approximately whites` attitudes towards blacks.

METHODOLOGY

Using responses of non-Hispanic white individuals withinside the 1998–2002 General Social Surveys (GSS) merged with yr 2000 Census information, we study contextual outcomes on 8 measures of racial angle that together constitute conventional prejudice; perceptions associated to "new" racism; and racial coverage perspectives.

1998–2002 General Social Survey Samples

General Social Surveys (GSS) are administered biannually to stratified, multi-degree samples of English-speak me Americans over the age of 17 with the aid of using the National Opinion Research Center (NORC) on the University of Chicago. The National Opinion Research Center is one of the few studies corporations that has retained the functionality to behavior countrywide surveys thru in-man or woman interviews, taken into consideration the gold widespread in survey studies. For this reason, and due to the fact the song document of the personnel is outstanding, General Social Survey information are extensively appeared to be of the very best quality. The GSS information are specifically treasured for this studies due to the fact they include a wealthy form of state-of-the-art and well-examined measures of racial attitudes. The stereotype measures, for example, advanced for an in advance unique GSS module on Intergroup Relations, are diffused sufficient to expose proof of racial stereotyping now no longer detectable with the aid of using conventional stereotype questions (Bobo and Kluegel 1991).

The 1998, 2000, and 2002 surveys have been decided on for this challenge due to their temporal proximity to the 2000 decennial census that supplied the information on respondents` communities. For those 3 surveys, reaction costs have been 76%, 70%, and 70%, respectively. Over the 3 years, the non-Hispanic whites whose responses are tested right here range 6323. The GSS exercise of administering decided on inquiries to random sub-samples of respondents, inclusion of a few measures in handiest one or survey years, and object-unique refusals go away us with smaller samples for any given analysis. Ns variety from 2904 to 5264.

For those 3 surveys, NORC randomly decided on respondents from a hundred Primary Sampling Units (PSUs), 70 metropolitan regions and 30 non-metropolitan counties.6 Details of the sampling plan are to be had withinside the General Social Surveys 1972–2002: Cumulative Codebook, disbursed with the aid of using the Roper Center for Public Opinion Research. The PSUs are the contextual gadgets representing localities in our analyses.

Dependent Variables

Responses to twenty-3 questions have been used for my part or in scales to yield 8 measures of race-associated perspectives and emotions. This set consists of measures of "conventional prejudice," measures associated to "new" sorts of racism (Kinder and Sanders 1996), and signs of race-coverage-associated perspectives.

Three scales constitute conventional prejudice: Stereotyping is the unweighted imply of 3 quantities, the variations in white respondents' scores of whites and blacks on seven-factor scales representing trait dimensions of intelligence, industriousness, and propensity to violence. Emotion is the imply of quantities, variations in said warm temperature or coldness felt towards whites and blacks, and variations in respondents` emotions of closeness towards whites and blacks. Social Distance is the imply of said reactions to dwelling in a half-black community and to having a near member of the family marry a black man or woman.

Three measures determine perceptions related with "new" sorts of racism. Attributions for Racial Inequality is a four-object scale registering respondents` undertaking of obligation for racial inequality to blacks` inborn ability, loss of effort, insufficient schools, and discrimination. Belief in Reverse Discrimination information respondents` tests of ways regularly white activity seekers lose out too much less certified blacks. Racial Resentment is an object scale registering sentiment that blacks ought to paintings their personal manner up and ought to now no longer push wherein they're now no longer wanted.

Finally, measures determine perspectives on racial coverage questions. Opposition to Affirmative Action information critiques approximately racial choices in hiring and promotion. Opposition to Government Help is a scale registering respondents` favored stage of presidency spending to help blacks and their critiques approximately whether or not the authorities is obliged to assist blacks.

Focal Predictors: Locality Characteristics

The focal predictors are constructed from facts accumulated withinside the 2000 census for the one hundred metropolitan and non-metropolitan GSS number one sampling units. Race Composition is a truthful degree of percentage of the populace this is African American. White Educational Composition is the share of white citizens who've now no longer attained a university degree, converted to a trendy score (to be withinside the equal metric because the monetary composition indicator defined next). White Economic Composition is a scale, the imply of trendy rankings representing the neighborhood percentage of whites falling underneath the poverty stage, the share having own circle of relative's earnings much less than $50,000, and the share of white guys who aren't employed. The percentage black withinside the neighborhood populace is correlated with the 2 SES signs at negligible levels (r = −.01 and r = −.12 for instructional and monetary composition, respectively); the 2 signs of white SES composition are greater strongly correlated with every other (r = .67). Note that the coding of those SES composition predictors, with excessive values assigned in which lower-fame whites predominate, approach we'd see high-quality relationships with racial prejudice if disparaging racial attitudes have been endorsed in which SES composition withinside the white network is low.

Locality-stage controls

Population Size, the herbal log of the 2000 populace be counted number for the locality, become protected in all analyses, as become Metro Status, coded 1 for metropolitan localities and zero for non-metropolitan counties. Region become represented via way of means of a variable South, coded 1 for Southern localities, zero otherwise.

Individual-stage controls

Four traits of person respondents have been protected in all analyses: Education, measured as years of schooling; Age in years; gender, categorized Male to suggest coding of adult males as 1, ladies as zero; and Family Income on a 23-factor scale. For structured measures protected in multiple survey 12 months, we additionally protected dummy variables to suggest 12 months of the survey, Year 2000 and Year 2002; 1998 become the reference 12 months.

Analyses

The multi-degree samples from which our GSS facts come, with survey respondents clustered in 100 geographical areas, name for specialized facts evaluation. Co-citizens of localities are probably greater just like every apart from to people randomly-picked from throughout the country, on an entire variety of unmeasured in addition to measured traits; greater technically, there may be a loss of independence amongst mistakes inside clusters. For our principal measures of network traits, all citizens from the equal locality have equal values. This undertaking employs the multi-stage modeling software HLM that adjusts for the shape of those facts (Raudenbush and Bryk 2002).7

Our method is first of all an evaluation that consists of Race Composition alongside person-stage and locality-stage controls. In Model 2 we upload the second one focal contextual predictor,

White Educational Composition. In Model 3, White Educational Composition is eliminated and White Economic Composition is added. Finally, Model four contains each White Educational Composition and White Economic Composition.8

HLM outcomes for the 4 units of analyses are supplied in Tables three and four. As background, results of character-stage traits at the 8 established measures are supplied in Table three for the version that protected all 3 focal contextual variables at the side of locality-stage controls (Model four in Table four). The character-stage results extrude little as contextual variables are brought to the version, and they may be now no longer the point of interest of this research; for this reason, the unmarried set of summaries supplied in Table three suffices. As discovered in in advance racial mindset research, extra exceptionally knowledgeable respondents provide extra revolutionary solutions to racial mindset questions.

On the social distance scale and mainly the 2 coverage opinion measures, after controlling on training whites with better own circle of relative's earnings had been extra negative. When the liberalizing has an effect on of the training that frequently accompanies better earnings is statistically removed, the ensuing partial results of own circle of relative's earnings may also imply that people with the maximum to lose, whether or not it's reputation, occupational position, or money, are maximum invested withinside the racial reputation quo. There became a gender distinction on 5 of the 8 established measures, in all instances girls being the extra revolutionary; proof for enormous gender variations in racial attitudes is inconsistent (see Hughes and Tuch, 2003). With one exception, the younger are extra revolutionary than older respondents, a not unusual place locating for a few forms of racial mindset measures (see e.g. Taylor 1998) frequently interpreted in cross-sectional statistics including those to be "cohort results," reflecting accepted racial perspectives on the time diverse cohorts got here of age.

Table four carries the facts this is our vital interest – contextual results for the localities that represent the GSS number one sampling units. As mentioned in advance, 3 environmental factors -- populace length, metro reputation, and region -- are protected in all analyses as controls. Status as a metropolitan region or non-metro county in no way made a distinction in those established measures, and not one of the sizeable results of populace length withstood the creation of locality-stage training withinside the analysis. Congruent with findings in different current research (see, for example, Tuch and Martin 1997), wherein we see proof of local variations, Southerners are the much less revolutionary group.

Effects of black populace percentage

As we see withinside the first column of Table four (representing Model 1), while Race composition is the best focal environmental predictor, it has exceptionally sizeable results on 5 of the 8 racial mindset measures. In all instances, the racial composition results are withinside the anticipated direction – detrimental attitudes (coded high) are extra not unusual place amongst non-Hispanic whites residing in regions wherein blacks constitute a bigger share of the populace.

Two of the mindset dimensions displaying non-sizeable results of black populace percentage are the Emotion scale and the Social Distance measure. Perhaps the superb emotions and recognition registered on those signs are so carefully tied to private revel in as to be noticeably impervious to environmental have an effect on.

Surprisingly, the best different size of racial attitudes now no longer suffering from share black became competition to affirmative motion.

Readers may also remember that opinion approximately affirmative motion became one of the few racial mindset objects that did display an impact of metro-stage racial proportions withinside the 1991 phone survey statistics analyzed with the aid of using Oliver and Mendelberg (2000), a sample the sooner researchers interpreted as reflecting racial hazard tied to metro-stage activity competition. Evidently that impact isn't always robust.

For the 5 dimensions of racial attitudes that confirmed a sizeable effect of race composition, results declined best modestly while the opposite focal contextual predictors had been added into the version (see columns 2–four in Table four). All remained without a doubt sizeable.

Education and financial dimensions of white socioeconomic composition

What approximately the effect of white academic composition on racial attitudes? Recall, we manage for the training of the character white respondents; we ask right here approximately the effect of the share of university graduates withinside the collectivity of neighborhood whites, over and above any effect of university at the attitudes of people who attended. Their personal training aside, do the ones residing wherein noticeably few whites keep university levels screen more race prejudice? Across our mostly-metro localities, a contextual impact of white academic composition is sizeable for 6 of the 8 racial mindset measures, prejudice being better in white groups wherein the university knowledgeable are noticeably rare. It is measures of conventional prejudice – stereotyping and emotion – which might be unaffected with the aid of using white academic composition.

When race composition and white academic composition are withinside the version together, which have an effect on is the more potent? The standardized slope coefficients11 supplied in parentheses for Model 2 in Table four inform the story, and the solution is mixed. Where there may be any distinction to talk of withinside the energy of the 2 environmental influences, racial composition has the more potent have an effect on stereotyping, at the same time as academic composition has the more potent have an effect on social distance, racial resentment, and competition to affirmative motion. The contextual predictors have sizeable and about similarly robust results on attributions for racial inequality, perception in opposite discrimination, and competition to authorities help; and neither has a sizeable impact on emotion.

In sum, internet of character white respondents` training, the academic composition of the white network is certainly a critical environmental have an effect on racial attitudes. In fact, on 3 dimensions of racial attitudes the have an effect on of white academic composition is appreciably more potent than they have an effect on of locality race composition. But how are we to interpret those results? Is white training stage a proxy for financial trouble amongst whites withinside the locality, as distinguished in advance researchers regarded to assume? The solution is obvious while we upload white financial reputation to the HLM analyses. For Model four, wherein all 3 focal contextual predictors are protected, the six results of white academic stage that had been sizeable in Model 2 stay sizeable.

In assessment to the Model four findings for academic composition, partial results of white financial composition are non-sizeable throughout the board. Does collinearity play a function right here? As mentioned in advance, the contextual training and financial signs are appreciably correlated with every different.

Is the absence of considerable white monetary composition consequences only a count of white training degree having stolen its thunder withinside the multivariate analysis? No. As found out via way of means of the coefficients for Model three, without white instructional composition withinside the analysis, white monetary composition has considerable consequences on 4 of the 8 dimensions of racial attitudes, however simplest at the .05 degree. Comparison of Model 2 and Model three standardized coefficients for the 2 environmental SES dimensions confirms that training is dominant, now no longer economics: The distinguished contextual training impact is simply that – now no longer a proxy for the impact of monetary composition. Indeed, the monetary composition of the white network appears to play no function in shaping racial attitudes as soon as instructional composition is controlled.

SUMMARY AND DISCUSSION

What have we found out from those records, and what questions want to be resolved? For a start, the race composition of the one hundred metropolitan regions and non-metro counties represented withinside the 1998–2002 General Social Surveys has an effect on 5 of the 8 dimensions of racial attitudes held via way of means of white citizens. In localities in which the black populace is notably large, white citizens have a tendency to be much less innovative on many styles of race-associated attitudes. This sample is congruent with claims of decided on in advance analysts, together with Taylor`s (1998) end primarily based totally on GSS records amassed a decade in advance. It is incongruent with Oliver and Mendelberg`s (2000) skepticism approximately the significance of black presence withinside the network, in all likelihood reflecting variations withinside the size of race composition, the structured measures, the sample, or their emphasis on zip code-degree consequences in place of the ones of large geographical units.

With admire to the prominence of white instructional composition as a contextual impact on white racial attitudes, Oliver and Mendelberg`s (2000) factor is made greater strongly via way of means of those consequences than via way of means of their own. At the metro- or non-metro-county degree, the percentage of whites without a university diploma surpasses black populace percentage withinside the consistency and length of its consequences on white attitudes.

Importantly, as visible in Table four consequences for Model four, whilst the contextual training and monetary signs are each protected withinside the analysis, white instructional composition stays a considerable predictor for maximum racial mindset measures and white monetary composition is by no means considerable. White instructional composition isn't always a proxy for fabric difficulty withinside the network: Relatively low fees of university training amongst white citizens are connected to terrible racial attitudes amongst whites; time-honored monetary difficulty withinside the white network has no such impact.

Data regulations restriction our cap potential to increase those analyses into the past, however it's far possibly that styles discovered right here are as a minimum to a point traditionally specific. Given the racial turbulence related to the northward migration via way of means of African Americans all through the primary 1/2 of the 20th century, parallel analyses of records from that generation would possibly properly have proven even greater dramatic responsiveness via way of means of northern whites to the dimensions of nearby black populations. The latest upward push of Hispanic populace withinside the U.S. and related public debate will offer a possibility to search for such converting styles withinside the future. In GSS and census facts from 1990, the effect of black populations on anti-black attitudes amongst whites observed no parallel withinside the affiliation of Latino populace figures with anti-Latino attitudes amongst Anglos (Taylor 1998). Given the cutting-edge bleak monetary picture, with media and political interest to Hispanic immigration at the upswing, we'd assume the nearby Latino populace percentage to have developing consequences at the attitudes of Anglos. This opportunity requires studies interest.

The effect of nearby white instructional composition on residents' racial attitudes can be aware of ancient alternate as well. Especially, values and norms associated with racial equality had been certainly promoted greater vigorously in faculties and universities all through and after the civil rights revolution won momentum withinside the Fifties and 1960s.

In short, country wide populace shifts, converting monetary conditions, political climate, and social actions probable have an effect on white response to each the race composition and the white instructional composition of nearby communities. We need to take the proof suggested right here as a picture of styles acquiring whilst the closing decennial census facts had been to be had.

This mission assessed loads of racial mindset measures, in acknowledgment that whites` racial views are regularly multi-dimensional, and styles that emerge in survey facts aren't always homogenous. Conclusions primarily based totally on a handful of racial attitudes are worrisome; extrade choices of attitudinal final results measures would possibly have yielded unique effects. The important findings of this look at are fairly uniform, despite the fact that there may be a few variant in discovered environmental impacts at the extrade measures of racial attitudes. Better expertise of this variability might be useful.

Many analysts of racial attitudes have drawn the difference among voicing popularity of racial minorities and helping modifications important to treatment racial inequity (see e.g. Jackman and Crane 1986; Schuman et al. 1997; Bobo and Kluegel 1997; Quillian 2006). It might be exciting and informative if environmental outcomes verified right here systematically differed whilst the final results measures assessed conventional prejudice in preference to coverage perspectives. Although effects throughout the 8 racial mindset measures used right here confirmed no such divide, destiny studies need to allow evaluation of the opportunity that environmental impacts perform otherwise for conceptually exclusive training of racial attitudes.

The provocative findings suggested right here underline the want to increase fuller perception into the mediation of the 2 contextual outcomes proven right here to be important—nearby black populace percentage and white instructional composition.

Beginning with the former, what methods in localities with huge black populations gas poor racial attitudes amongst whites? As cited withinside the creation to this paper, hazard related with "sensible organization conflict" (Levine and Campbell 1972; Blalock 1967) or slippage of "organization position" (Blumer 1958) is regularly presumed to be the important thing mediator. However, in advance efforts to illustrate such mediation have now no longer been persuasive (Fossett and Kiecolt 1989; Taylor 1998).

Attempts to validate hazard interpretations of race composition outcomes are complex through the ability life of many kinds of hazard – monetary, political, fame, physical, cultural, and "diffuse hazard to the social order" (Stults and Baumer 2007). Also, hazard exists in the attention of the beholder, and belief isn't always veridical. Interpreting their man or woman-degree facts, Halperin, Pedahzur, and Canetti-Nisim (2007) confront this fact, suggesting that superior schooling can also additionally decrease hostility closer to outgroups through reducing the belief of hazard. An analogous factor changed into powerfully made through Kinder and Sanders: "Threat isn't always a lot a clear-eyed belief as it's miles an emotion-weighted down mindset. Whites experience racially threatened due to the fact they're predisposed to study the sector that way; they see hazard and danger whilst others, greater sympathetic of their racial sentiments, do now no longer" (1996: 90). These demanding situations to expertise the mental mediation of white reactions to massive black populations need to energize instead of deter studies.

Also, as cited in Taylor (1998), the look for mediators that translate nearby demographic realities into residents` racial perspectives need to now no longer be restrained to perceived hazard and different mental states of mind. The content material of nearby broadcast and print media need to surely be channels thru which race composition comes to steer white attitudes. The shape of nearby political opposition and public statements of applicants and nearby officers are different ability mediators open to exam through active researchers. Important paintings stay to be done.

What approximately the contextual schooling impact? The 1998–2002 GSS facts really display that white instructional composition isn't always a proxy for monetary composition in its effect on racial attitudes. Since instructional and now no longer monetary fame makes a difference, scapegoating developing from traumatic environment isn't always a viable mediator—we need to appearance elsewhere. How do low charges of university attainment amongst nearby whites, internet of man or woman schooling, translate into much less favorable attitudes closer to blacks?

The content material of nearby norms changed into discounted as a proof through Oliver and Mendelberg (2000), who reasoned that the technology of robust norms might require sustained interpersonal interplay now no longer discovered throughout huge localities. Their locating that the power of the schooling impact did now no longer growth with respondents` duration of house withinside the identical network changed into additionally taken as disqualifying proof for the norms-as-mediator notion. Indeed, for the 2002 GSS facts we had been capable of search for the identical cross-degree moderation, and prefer the sooner researchers didn`t discover proof for it (effects to be had from the author).

But consider Moore and Ovadia`s (2006) thinking. Focusing on higher-knowledgeable localities wherein modern efforts can be released in preference to on poorly-knowledgeable groups wherein white prejudice can be socially supported, those analysts argue that sustained interpersonal touch amongst citizens isn't always essential to generate high-quality environmental impact. Rather, the solution may also lie in "institutional and macrosocial means" (2006:2215). Where there's an essential mass of the higher knowledgeable whites proven right here and someplace else to have extra high-quality racial attitudes, localities may also extra regularly by skip and put into effect anti-discrimination laws, definitely constitute racial range in college curricula and civic programs, and usually aid messages of tolerance and intergroup appreciation. Effects of this network way of life could be felt through surprisingly-knowledgeable and poorly-knowledgeable white citizens alike.

1The battle among those styles and claims that touch can enhance intergroup family members is extra obvious than real. Locales with huge proportions of African American citizens regularly have excessive ranges of residential segregation, precluding the form of intergroup touch discovered to inspire high-quality mindset change (All port 1954).

3Taking off from Oliver and Mendelberg (2000), next research through Oliver and his collaborators have included Hispanic and Asian-American presence as capacity environmental predictors and feature broadened the set of established measures examined. Also, degree of evaluation has moved to middle stage: Oliver and Wong (2003), in conjunction with Ha (2010), finish that extensive outgroup illustration withinside the community encourages high-quality attitudes amongst citizens, whilst a huge outgroup populace withinside the metropolitan location appear to have a bad impact on attitudes.

4It can be instructive that Moore and Ovadia`s dialogue shifts among reference to "attitudes" and reference to "norms." Schuman et al. (1997:2–5) offer a considerate reaction to critics who fear that race mindset measures may also in large part mirror survey respondents` deference to assumed normative expectancies held through researchers, particularly in face-to-face interviews and amongst surprisingly knowledgeable respondents. Debates approximately what mindset measures clearly degree are too complicated to be notably taken into consideration right here. However, the Schuman et al. argument that norms exert effective effects on social existence means that if certainly racial mindset measures are partly barometers of racial norms, they nevertheless deliver us with very essential information.

Another benefit of analyzing context consequences for large geographical devices is that there's much less purpose to fear approximately the course of causation among race composition and attitudes. The fowl and egg hassle haunts contextual in addition to individual-degree tests of the effect of proximity and phone on intergroup attitudes. Although information analytic techniques were hired to provide a few warranty that choice of numerous environments isn't always the number one motive of obvious touch consequences (see for instance Branton and Jones 2005; Dixon 2006; Welch et al. 2001) maximum analysts renowned that opposite causality stays an issue (Oliver and Mendelberg 2000). The function of race composition in white Americans` community alternatives is indisputable (see, for instance, Zubrinsky Charles 2001, 2006), however it's far probably that financial considerations, sentiment, and twist of fate dominate people`s choice of metropolitan location or non-metropolitan county. For maximum whites, the financial or sentimental price of fending off a metropolitan location due to its minority populace could be too great. And ranges of residential segregation are excessive sufficient in certainly all areas (Massey and Denton 1993; Stoll 2005) in order that the ones averse to range can fulfill their flavor for racially homogenous neighborhoods with inside the metropolitan location they pick for different reasons.

9Southern location and percentage black are confounded (r=.581), and the racial records of the U.S. leaves a few query approximately a way to disentangle the 2. Inclusion of every in a multivariate evaluation of white racial attitudes commonly weakens the discovered effect of the opposite. The location results visible for Model 1 must be interpreted remembering that they may be partial results, controlling on black populace percentage (in addition to populace length and metro status).

The corollary of the factor made in Note 6 is that assessing the effect of percentage black on white attitudes after controlling for Southern location, as we did right here, predictably yields conservative estimates. If the paradox approximately the precise remedy of location and race composition in multivariate analyses were resolved through reporting race composition coefficients without the manipulate for South, we'd see extensively large percentage black results on maximum established measures; and for one of the 3 mindset measures that didn`t display a massive impact of percentage black in Table 4, social distance, the impact will become massive at p consequences to be had from the authors).

Standardized slope coefficients are supplied in parentheses for all results said in Tables three and due to the fact they permit assessment of the power of the numerous partial results. They may be interpreted because the alternate in standardized established variable ratings anticipated whilst the impartial variable will increase through one general deviation, controlling for different variables with inside the model.

As stated earlier, Oliver and Mendelberg (2000) cautioned that residential segregation may also alleviate perceived hazard in localities wherein blacks constitute a massive percentage of the populace, mitigating the tendency for terrible racial attitudes to develop. In supplementary evaluation we observed most effective certified guide for this hypothesis: For the stereotyping and emotion measures, the effect of race composition changed into appreciably weaker in metro regions wherein the (dissimilarity) segregation index changed into high; however, the interplay changed into now no longer massive for the opposite six mindset measures, and for 5 of the six it ran with inside the contrary direction. Interaction results among residential segregation and the 2 socioeconomic composition measures have been much more likely to run with inside the anticipated direction, socioeconomic composition results being fainter whilst segregation changed into high, however most effective of the 16 interplay results have been massive. (Full consequences are to be had from the author.)

For decades, race students have requested whether or not the tendency for the higher knowledgeable to present extra liberal solutions on surveys represented their more dedication to racial equality or something instead extra superficial, even self-serving (see e.g. Jackman and Muha 1984). The instructional composition impact said right here isn't always open to the identical questions: If citizens of white groups with a better percentage of university graduates seem extra liberal throughout the board, the notably knowledgeable and the poorly knowledgeable alike, something extra considerable have to be occurring than a veneer of liberalism polished through university education.

Other critical questions, now no longer our consciousness right here, additionally deserve persevering with studies attention. We agree with destiny research will allow analysts to make assured statements approximately variations in contextual affects throughout broader and narrower contextual units, and to increase generalizations approximately environmental results to multi-racial and multi-ethnic perceivers and targets.

CPSIA information can be obtained
at www.ICGtesting.com
Printed in the USA
LVHW052325140523
746973LV00003B/318